DARLINGTON
IN OLD PHOTOGRAPHS

———— COLLECTED BY ————
GEORGE FLYNN

ALAN SUTTON
1989

Alan Sutton Publishing
Gloucester

First published 1989

British Library Cataloguing in Publication Data

Darlington in old photographs.
1.   Durham (County). Darlington, history
I.   Flynn, George, *1929–*
942.8'63

ISBN 0–86299–585–X

Typesetting and origination by
Alan Sutton Publishing
Printed in Great Britain by
Dotesios Printers Limited

CONTENTS

INTRODUCTION

Although the principles of the camera obscura, by which an image could be projected, and the properties of certain light-sensitive chemicals had been known since the seventeenth century, it was not until 1827 that Joseph Nicéphore Niépce, a French artist and technical inventor, succeeded in making a permanent image of the view from the window of his attic. After his death in 1833, it was left to his partner, Louis Daguerre, to refine and perfect the process and, in 1839, he displayed the results of his experiments to members of the Académie des Sciences and the Académie des Beaux Arts in Paris.

Quite independently of Niépce and Daguerre, William Henry Fox Talbot of Lacock Abbey, Wiltshire had been experimenting with the photographic image since 1834 and examples of his 'photogenic drawings' were exhibited at the Royal Institution in 1839. He also read a paper on his process to the Royal Society. The age of the 'mechanical sketchbook' had arrived. Frederick Scott Archer's wet collodion process, unveiled at the Great Exhibition of 1851, was to oust both the Daguerrotype and Fox Talbot's Calotype and was to be used to bring home to the general public the horrors of the Crimean campaign and the American Civil War.

Twenty years later, Richard Leach Maddox's experiments produced the gelatin dry plate which simplified photographic technique and was to lead to a revolution in camera design.

An American bank clerk, George Eastman, who took up photography as a hobby in 1877 and established his own company to manufacture dry plates four years later, brought photography within the reach of millions with the production of the first Kodak camera in 1888. Launched with the advertising slogan 'You press the button, we do the rest', the camera, which took 100 circular exposures on a roll of paper film, was simply sent to Eastman's factory for processing and was returned, reloaded with a new film. It was the beginning of the era of 'point and shoot' photography.

In Great Britain, the demand for photographic views and street scenes was stimulated by the Postmaster General's decision in September 1894 to permit the sending of picture postcards through Her Majesty's Mail. Many of the resulting photographs were of high quality, but views were often 'improved' by painting out unattractive details, such as industrial chimneys and tramwires, and substituting clouds. Mistakes were sometimes made with the captions, streets being wrongly named, and it was not unknown for a view to be printed the wrong way round. Nevertheless, these postcard photographers (many of them unknown) and publishers have left us an irreplaceable historical record of life in Britain from the turn of the century onwards.

Darlington, described by the sixteenth-century antiquarian, John Leland, as 'the best market town in the bishopric, saving Durham' has been an important centre of trade, at least since the end of the twelfth century, when the lord of the manor, the Bishop of Durham, granted the town borough status and the right to hold a market. The town's economy was based on the sale of wool, the production of woollen cloth and the preparation of leather, a by-product of its important cattle market. Darlington's linen manufactory, for which it was to become nationally famous, appears to have had its origins in the sixteenth century at a time when the production of woollen cloth seems to have been in temporary decline. By the middle of the eighteenth century, although Darlington had a thriving woollen industry, the town was renowned for its huckaback, a linen fabric used in the making of tablecloths and napkins, which was manufactured in a variety of widths. Great quantities were sent to London, 'the broad sort being made no where else in England'.

Situated as it was on the main eastern route between London and Scotland, Darlington became a recognized stopping place for travellers. Both Edward I and Edward III are known to have stayed in the town on their journeys north during their campaigns against the Scots. In 1502, Margaret, the eldest daughter of Henry VII, stayed overnight in the bishop's manor house in Darlington on her way to Scotland to marry James IV. It was during a visit to the bishopric in 1617 that Margaret's great-grandson, James I of England and VI of Scotland is reputed to have made his uncomplimentary remark about the town. On being told that he had arrived at 'Darnton', he is said to have replied, 'Darnton! – Humph! – I think it's Darnton i' t' Dirt!' The state of the town's approach roads left much to be desired, dusty and rutted in summer, a morass in the winter. Even after roads were turnpiked in the latter half of the eighteenth century, lack of funds often left roads unrepaired. The road between Stockton and Darlington was made passable by throwing tree trunks into the ruts, and in the winter of 1811 a resident of Rushyford recorded the loss of seven horses, whose legs had been broken on the rough road between Durham and Darlington.

By 1801, the population of the town, estimated to have been about 3,200 in the mid-eighteenth century, had risen to 4,670. The mechanization of the spinning of both woollen and linen yarn had increased the demand for hand-loom weavers and it was estimated that some 1,500 looms were employed in Darlington and its surrounding villages before the advent of the power-loom.

The opening of the Stockton & Darlington Railway in September 1825 to facilitate the transport of coal from the south-west Durham mines paved the way for the development of heavy engineering and iron and steel production in the town. Small foundries sprang up in the Hopetown area, in close proximity to the railway line. By 1841, the town's population had risen to 11,035. The arrival of the Great North of England Railway line, which was eventually to link London with Newcastle, encouraged the establishment of several iron-making works in the Albert Hill area between 1853 and 1864, and the opening of the railway locomotive building and repair works at North Road in 1863 attracted other railway-related industries to the town. The population increased dramatically: 1871 – 27,730; 1901 – 44,511; 1931 – 72,086; 1961 – 84,184.

Today, although its engineering base has been drastically reduced and its claim to being a 'railway' town now rests principally on its possession of a main-line station, Darlington 'the birthplace of railways', its boundaries extended by the Local Government Act of 1974, has a population of over 100,000 people.

Market Area, Victoria Road and Bank Top

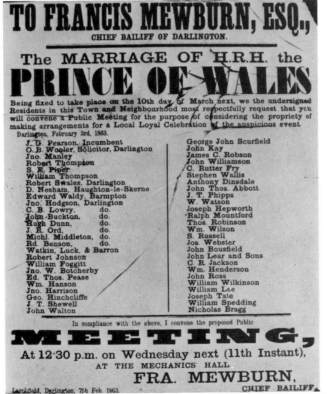

TO FRANCIS MEWBURN, ESQ.,

CHIEF BAILIFF OF DARLINGTON.

The **MARRIAGE OF H.R.H.** the

PRINCE OF WALES

Being fixed to take place on the 10th day of March next, we the undersigned Residents in this Town and Neighbourhood most respectfully request that you will convene a Public Meeting for the purpose of considering the propriety of making arrangements for a Local Loyal Celebration of the auspicious event.

Darlington, February 3rd, 1863.

J. G. Pearson, Incumbent	George John Scurfield
O. B. Wooler, Solicitor, Darlington	John Kay
Jno. Manley	James C. Robson
Robert Thompson	John Williamson
S. E. Piper	C. Rutter Fry
William Thompson	Stephen Wallis
Robert Swales, Darlington	Anthony Dinsdale
D. Nesham, Haughton-le-Skerne	John Thos. Abbott
Edward Waldy, Barmpton	J. T. Phipps
Jno. Hodgson, Darlington	W. Watson
C. B. Lowry, do.	Joseph Hepworth
John Buckton, do.	Ralph Mountford
Hugh Dunn, do.	Thos. Robinson
J. R. Ord, do.	Wm. Wilson
Michl. Middleton, do.	S. Russell
Rd. Benson, do.	Jos. Webster
Watkin, Luck, & Barron	John Bousfield
Robert Johnson	John Lear and Sons
William Foggitt	C. R. Jackson
Jno. W. Botcherby	Wm. Henderson
Ed. Thos. Pease	John Ross
Wm. Hanson	William Wilkinson
Jno. Harrison	William Lee
Geo. Hinchcliffe	Joseph Tate
J. T. Shewell	William Spedding
John Walton	Nicholas Bragg

In compliance with the above, I convene the proposed Public

MEETING,

At 12·30 p.m. on Wednesday next (11th Instant),
AT THE MECHANICS' HALL.

FRA. MEWBURN,
CHIEF BAILIFF.

Larchfield, Darlington, 7th Feb. 1863.

BEFORE DARLINGTON BECAME A CORPORATE BOROUGH in 1867, the main authority in the town was the Borough Bailiff, who had the power to convene public meetings. In 1863, when some of the town's influential citizens wished to discuss ways of celebrating the marriage of the future King Edward VII, Francis Mewburn, the last Borough Bailiff of the town, was called upon to exercise this power.

IN THE TWELFTH CENTURY the Bishop of Durham granted Darlington the right to hold a market. The market tolls, from which the freeholders of the town were exempted, formed part of the bishop's revenue. Later, the collection of tolls was leased out to persons willing to make a lump sum payment to the bishop. In 1856, the town bought the market rights for £7,800. This photograph was taken c. 1910.

Bottom, right.
BANK HOLIDAY MONDAYS meant closed shops as well as closed banks in most towns and cities until the late 1960s. This was not so in Darlington, where the Bank Holiday market was a great attraction, not only to townspeople but also to those who lived in a wide surrounding area. This 1930s scene shows some of the crowds who came to Darlington to enjoy a day out, visiting the shops and stalls.

BEFORE THE EARLY 1920s (although there were a few stalls selling general merchandise, ice-cream and sweets), the Monday open market in Darlington catered mainly for the farming community. This photograph of 1922 shows the Bakehouse Hill side of the Market Place: Thomas Pease's wine and spirit shop, the Bull's Head Hotel and Mason's Dining Rooms. While the occupiers and usage may have changed (e.g. the Bull's Head lost its licence in 1956), the buildings are still clearly recognizable today.

13

THE LICENSEE JOHN CLARKE and his family posed on the doorstep of the Market Hotel in Bakehouse Hill in 1890. Later, after two extensions, the public house became known as the Market Tavern, with yet another change of name in 1982 to the Pennyweight.

THE TOWN CLOCK TOWER, which is one of the most prominent buildings in Darlington, was designed, along with the market building, by the nationally-known architect, Alfred Waterhouse. Completed in 1864, the clock, with its five bells, was given to the town by Joseph Pease. Its original coloured dial was later changed to make its hands and figures easier to see.

WHEN THE COVERED MARKET was opened at 7.00 a.m. on 2 May 1864, Mr J. Wrightson of the Sun Inn (Prospect Place) had the distinction of being the first customer, by buying a leg of mutton. The interior layout of the market, seen here in the 1930s, was altered drastically in the 1978 refurbishment.

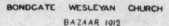

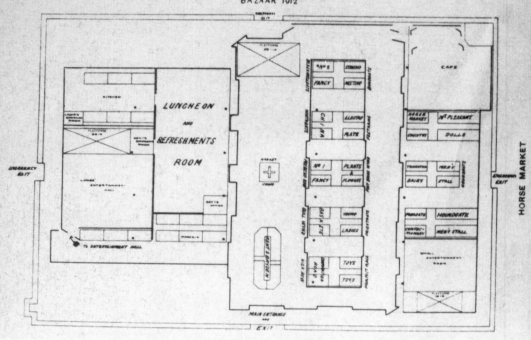

OCCASIONALLY THE COVERED MARKET has been used for purposes other than the sale of produce. This plan shows the layout of the Bondgate Wesleyan Church's Centenary Bazaar, held 26–29 November 1912. The 1727 market cross, shown in the centre of the plan, was placed in the market hall in 1864. Removed in 1955, the town is still awaiting its promised re-erection in a suitable place.

THIS VIEW OF THE HORSEMARKET SIDE OF THE MARKET PLACE, taken in the 1950s, shows a line of Darlington's original, elegant electric lamp standards. From right to left can also be seen: the Hole in the Wall and the Waterloo public houses, the Broadway Cafe, A. & M. Harland (tobacconists), and the council's Weights and Measures Department, housed in the former Dolphin Hotel. The canopies on the north, east and south sides of the market hall were added in 1885, to increase the covered space available for stallholders.

DARLINGTON WAS 'EN FÊTE' in June 1895 on the occasion of the visit of the Duke and Duchess of York (later King George V and Queen Mary). Their Royal Highnesses came to the town to visit the Royal Agricultural Show which was held at Hummersknott. The duke and duchess's projected stay at Raby Castle had to be cancelled, owing to the indisposition of Lord Barnard. Lord and Lady Londonderry nobly stepped into the breach and offered the hospitality of Wynyard Hall.

THE ROYAL COUPLE had processed from Bank Top station through Parkgate, Bondgate, Stanhope Road and Blackwellgate before making their appearance on the platform erected to accommodate 200 people in front of the old Town Hall. The town clerk, F.T. Steavenson, read an address of welcome to which the duke suitably replied. The 1st Volunteer Battalion of the Durham Light Infantry provided most of the Guard of Honour.

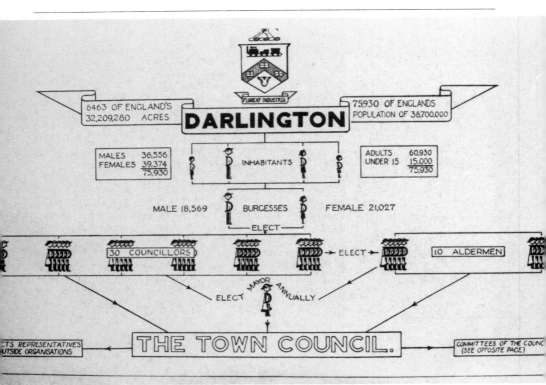

IN THE INTER-WAR YEARS, Darlington Corporation issued a booklet giving details of its various departments which served the townspeople. This chart, from the 1937 edition, gives a graphic display of the town's statistics, 'D' for Darlington being amusingly incorporated into the little drawings.

SINCE RECEIVING CORPORATE BOROUGH STATUS in 1867, the town has had a mayor. The Pease family, which played a major part in Darlington's affairs, provided five mayors before 1900. This photograph is of Henry Fell Pease (1838–96) of Brinkburn, who was the town's chief citizen on two occasions, 1874–5 and 1894–5. H.F. Pease, who was also MP for Cleveland 1885–96, married Elizabeth Mary, the daughter of John Beaumont Pease of North Lodge.

AS WELL AS ACHIEVING corporate borough status in 1867, Darlington also acquired the right to elect its own Member of Parliament. Edmund Backhouse (1824–1906) was returned as the first MP for the town in 1868, a position he was to hold until 1880. In 1850 he sold Polam, which he had inherited on his father's death, and moved to Middleton Tyas. In 1897, he retired to Trebah, near Falmouth in Cornwall, where he died.

THE LATE EDMUND BACKHOUSE,

OUR FIRST M.P.

Printed and Published by Mawson, Phillips, & Co., Ld., Sunderland. [Entered at Stationer's Ha

BORN IN BRISTOL, Theodore Fry married Sophia, the daughter of John Pease of East Mount, in 1862. In 1866, the Frys returned to Darlington to live at Woodburn (the name of their former house in Bristol), one of the two houses John Pease built at Salutation Corner for his daughters. In 1880 Fry was elected as MP for Darlington and remained the town's representative until 1895, when he was defeated by Arthur Pease. After Sophia Fry died in 1897, Theodore remarried and moved to Caterham, where he died in 1912.

THIS STONE, built into the wall of a shop at the corner of Bull Wynd and Horsemarket, depicts the shovel-tailed bull, the crest of the Bulmer family. The stone is mentioned in documents of 1666 and again in 1760 when John Pease, a grocer, bought 'the burgage called le Bull at one side of Bull Wynd adorned with the Bulmer crest'.

NEW CENTRAL HALL,
Darlington.

ADDRESS

TO THE RIGHT HONORABLE

SIR ROBERT PEEL, Bart., M.P.

SIR ROBERT PEEL has consented to come into the Town of Darlington, on his way to Wynyard, by the Express Train at 5 o'Clock on the Afternoon of WEDNESDAY next, (September 1st), and the ADDRESS will be presented at the NEW CENTRAL HALL, by JOSEPH PEASE, Esq., immediately on his arrival.

Sir Robert's arrival at the Railway Station, will be announced to the Town by the hoisting of the Union Jack on the top of the Central Hall, and by a Peal on the Bells.

The Platform in the Hall will be reserved for those immediately connected with the presentation, and the Gallery and a portion of the Hall for Ladies having Tickets.

The entrance to the Hall, both for Carriages and those on Foot, will be solely by the door in the Market Place, and the side door at the Market Place end of the Wynd, EXCEPT FOR PARTIES HAVING PLATFORM TICKETS WHO ARE TO ENTER AT THE MAIN DOOR IN THE WYND.

☞ All Carriages are to set down in the Market Place.

IT IS HOPED THE INHABITANTS WILL CLOSE THEIR SHOPS AT FOUR O'CLOCK.

Darlington, August 30th, 1847.

DARLINGTON: PRINTED AT THE OFFICE OF COATES AND FARMER.

DESIGNED BY JOHN MIDDLETON, a Darlington architect, the Central Buildings were opened in June 1847 to provide the inhabitants of the town with a public meeting place where alcohol was not sold. One of the earliest events to be held there was a visit by Sir Robert Peel on 1 September 1847. Sir Robert replied to Joseph Pease's address of welcome, expressing his 'sincerest wishes for the prosperity of the town and neighbourhood of Darlington.'

THIS MARKET DAY VIEW of the 1930s was taken from the balcony of the town clock, looking over the Leadyard towards Bank Top railway station. The densely packed rows of houses in Pensbury Street, Hargreave Terrace, Park Place, Park Street and Backhouse Street form ranks in front of the station.

THE CHURCH OF ST CUTHBERT, ignored by so many of the townspeople of Darlington, should be regarded as the town's most important building from architectural, historical and religious points of view. Built on the site of an earlier church, the present structure dates from 1192 and was the only building of public worship in the town until the Society of Friends registered a meeting house in 1689.

THE MOSAIC REREDOS behind the altar in St Cuthbert's Church was designed by John Dobbin, a London artist, in memory of his Darlington parents, John and Elizabeth, and his wife, Amey. When presented to the church in 1875, it was found to be too tall to fit under the sill of the east window and 2 ft of the picture had to be cut away.

FOR MANY YEARS the Leadyard, south of St Cuthbert's churchyard, was used as the town's 'country' bus station, serving the surrounding villages and towns. The bishop's medieval manor house, which had occupied the river end of this site until its demolition in 1870, had served as the town's workhouse since the early-eighteenth century. The building in the centre of this 1950s photograph, once the boardroom of the workhouse, became a Unitarian chapel and then a bus parcels office. On the right can be seen the Clarence Commercial Hotel. The whole site was cleared to make way for the Town Hall of 1970.

WHEN THE NEW UNITED BUS STATION in Feethams was opened in 1961, the Leadyard became a public car park. The old Pease house on the corner of the Leadyard and Feethams, seen in this 1960s photograph, was used as offices by Scotts Greys coaches, the Market Inspector, the Health Department and as a school clinic.

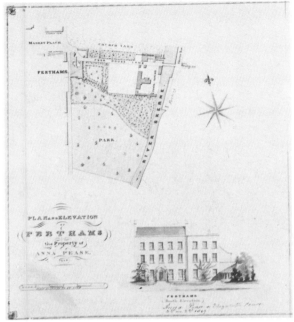

THIS PLAN OF 1849 shows the house called Feethams and its grounds, then the home of Anne Pease, the second wife of Joseph Pease (d. 1846), who was the younger brother of Edward, 'the father of railways'. The elevation depicts the south front of this early eighteenth-century house, which was reputed to be the largest dwelling house in the borough when it was first built.

THE STREET NOW CALLED FEETHAMS was originally the private drive to the house of the same name. After the Corporation purchased the house and grounds in the 1880s, part of the park, Feethams Field, was used for fairs, open-air auctions and the occasional display such as 'Meet the Army' shown here. The field is now covered by the Victoria Road roundabout.

CONGESTION CAUSED BY BUSES is nothing new in Darlington. In this early 1930s picture, at least eight petrol and trolley buses are vying with the pedestrians for passage along Horsemarket. The occasional car and horse-drawn cart adds to the chaotic market-day scene.

THE FEETHAMS GROUND of the Darlington Cricket and Athletic Club dates from 1866, when the site was first rented from John Beaumont Pease. The pavilion was opened in May 1906 by E.D. Walker.

DARLINGTON

Cricket & Athletic Club.

(President, E. D. WALKER, Esq., J.P.)

FEETHAM'S GROUND.

THIS is one of the Finest Athletic Grounds in the Kingdom, and is the Popular Resort of the Town. It is used extensively for Cricket, Tennis and Football. Athletic and Cycling Sports.

THIS ADVERTISEMENT from the early 1930s for the 'Feetham's Ground' was included in a guide produced to show the amenities of Darlington.

A PHOTOGRAPHER'S POSTCARD, *c.* 1910, with St Cuthbert's Church framed by young trees on Victoria Embankment. The factory chimney, to the left of the church, belonged to Pease's Mill, Priestgate.

ALTHOUGH MANY OF THE BUILDINGS on the south side of Victoria Road were demolished to make way for a dual carriageway, most of these substantial Victorian terraced houses on the north side still survive as office accommodation.

DESPITE THE LOSS OF BAY PLATFORMS and the implementation of British Rail's 'open access' policy, Bank Top station, built by the North Eastern Railway Company in 1887, still retains much of its original appearance and layout. In this picture, the NER seems to have hung flags from every available tie bar to celebrate the signing of the Armistice with Germany in November 1918.

SECTION TWO

Tubwell Row, Parkgate and Yarm Road

TWO GENTLEMEN DISCUSS the fate of the nation, while others congregate around the drinking fountain which stood at the top of Tubwell Row until 1903, when the laying of lines for the electric tram service necessitated its removal. The buildings on the right-hand side of the picture are today virtually the same as when the photograph was taken in around 1900.

THE BAY WINDOWS of the Queen's Head Hotel can be seen on the left of this 1890s photograph. The pump, seen in the middle of the street opposite Church Row, provided water for the beasts that were sold on market days. This pump is reputed to have been on the site of the original tub-well which gave the street its name. (It would be interesting to know why a mangle has been left at the kerbside.)

OUTSIDE THE TUBWELL ROW PREMISES of T. Gill, baker and noted pork pie maker, stand two horse-drawn traps, one with a baker's basket on top. The buildings were demolished to make way for the North Eastern Co-operative department store, which in turn is to be replaced by the Cornmill shopping development.

ALTHOUGH THE 1930s saw an increase in the number of motor vehicles, horse-drawn vehicles were still in use. The Savings Bank, the second building on the right, is now the office of the Britannic Assurance Company in Tubwell Row.

DARLINGTON ENTHUSIASTICALLY SUPPORTED the Lifeboat Saturday processions. The 1906 procession included the float of H. Foster and Sons, builders' merchants, showing the latest design in fireplaces, followed by a pipe band and a troop of Scouts. In the background the Borough Accountant's office can be seen. This became the Darlington Museum in 1921.

PREPARATORY WORK for the expansion of the North Eastern Co-operative Society store in the late 1960s, prior to rebuilding, briefly exposed the west side of Raby Hotel Yard before it too was flattened by bulldozers. The Co-operative buildings were themselves demolished in 1988.

THIS SHOT OF THE STONE BRIDGE over the River Skerne in the early 1890s shows the pronounced hump in the centre. When this bridge was replaced by a metal bridge in 1895, the opportunity was taken to widen the carriageway.

THE STONE BRIDGE of 1767 over the Skerne replaced an ancient bridge of nine arches. The reduction to three arches, constricting the flow of water, was said to have been the cause of the frequent floods in the Parkgate and Clay Row areas. A contributory factor must also have been the practice of dumping rubbish in the river, which can be seen to be blocking the right-hand side arch. This photograph must have been taken shortly after the disastrous fire of February 1894 at Pease's Mill, which can be seen, roofless, in the background.

THE NAG'S HEAD in Tubwell Row is another of Darlington's old-established inns. This photograph was taken at the turn of the century, when E.H. Ditchburn was the proprietor of this fine house. Reputed to be of seventeenth-century origin, the building was thought to be one of the most historically important in the town. This fact did not save it from demolition in 1962, to make way for an indifferent modern building. The shop on the left belonged to J. Goodwill.

THE DARLINGTON OPERA HOUSE AND EMPIRE LTD. was the original owner of what is now the council-owned Darlington Civic Theatre. On opening in September 1907 the theatre was not given the name of the owning company, but called the New Hippodrome and Palace of Varieties. Both of these names can be seen in this 1910 photograph of the building when 'The Great La Milo' was the star attraction.

Left.

THE SOUTH AFRICAN WAR MEMORIAL was unveiled on 5 August 1905 by Field Marshal Earl Roberts, who was made the first Freeman of the Borough on the same day. The statue had been the subject of much criticism in the town. It was said to be too aggressive, to have an awkward stance, and its base should have been made in one piece. Prior's Terrace, on the east side of the river, can be seen in the background.

A SCOUT GANG SHOW, 'Spotlight on the Gang', was first produced in Darlington in 1949 by Horace Robinson. The first show was held in Eastbourne School, but the next production moved to the Hippodrome, with a cast of over a hundred and more than twenty scene changes. Lady Starmer, who was a keen supporter of the shows, always provided ice-cream for those taking part. This photograph is of the 1950 show.

THE WHEATSHEAF HOTEL, a Newcastle Breweries Blue Star public house, occupied the corner of Skerne Row and Bridge Street. The name and licence were transferred to the new Wheatsheaf Hotel on Yarm Road in the mid-1930s.

TWO VIEWS OF BRIDGE STREET in the 1930s, which once ran from Park Street to Skerne Row on the eastern side of the river, and then to the footbridge at the bottom of the Leadyard. The footpath between the present-day police and fire stations now follows the route of Bridge Street. In the top picture, Binns' department store on High Row can be seen in the distance.

PARKGATE AND HIPPODROME, DARLINGTON.

SINGLE-DECK TRAMCAR No. 14 running along Parkgate towards the Hippodrome and St Hilda's Church in the early 1920s. On the right-hand side, confectionery could be bought at R.W. Hampton's shop and also at Lily Stoddart's, who sold Dainty Dinah toffee from Chester-le-Street.

'TRACKLESS TRAMS' began to replace the electric trams from March 1928. Trolley bus No. 23, shown here in Parkgate in 1930, has been stopped by the usual mishap of one or both of the trolley poles leaving the overhead wires. Trolley bus No. 22 passes the Greyhound Hotel on the other side.

ONE OF THE VEHICLES necessary to service the trolley bus system was the overhead repair van. This had an extending platform on the rear to enable the engineers to rectify faults in the wiring, connections, or the points at junctions in the system.

IF YOU WANTED Spratt's Dog Cakes or a bunch of bananas in 1913, then R. Stainthorp's shop in Parkgate was the place to go. He was well-known in the north-east, and apparently further afield, as a judge at bird shows.

ALTHOUGH THE SUFFIX 'GATE' in the names of the ancient thoroughfares of Darlington signifies 'street', the name of Parkgate is derived from the fact that the entrance to the bishop's Low Park on the banks of the Skerne was once here. J. Wilks and Co were house furnishers, and some of the shops on the right-hand side look the same today as in this 1910 postcard.

DARLINGTON'S FIRE BRIGADE moved from under the market hall in 1905 to its new premises in Borough Road, which were opened with a gold key by Councillor Oliver, the Chairman of the Fire Brigade Committee. As well as stabling for the fire-engine and horses, housing was also provided for the paid firemen. The houses on the left of this picture are soon to be demolished to make way for extensions to the Civic Theatre.

THE BOROUGH FIREMEN, resplendent in shining boots and brass helmets, were often in demand for processions and civic funerals. The brigade, under the command of Captain John Porritt, is seen to good effect in this 1925 picture.

DARLINGTON'S FIRE BRIGADE was founded in 1837, when a hand-worked pump was purchased by public subscription. Joseph Pease presented a horse-drawn steam fire-engine in the 1870s, and another was bought in 1898. The next major step was the purchase of a motorized engine in 1920 for £1,965. This 1920s photograph shows four appliances on display in Borough Road.

A HORSE-DRAWN ACCIDENT AMBULANCE was provided in 1905 by public subscription, prior to which road or works accident victims had to be conveyed to hospital by whatever transport was available. The ambulance was housed at the fire station in Borough Road. In the 1920s, the body of the vehicle was transferred to a Model T Ford chassis, and became popularly known as the 'Flying Bedstead'.

DURING THE SECOND WORLD WAR, all civic fire brigades were placed under the control of the National Fire Service. In this 1940s photograph, the Darlington Section of the NFS displays the produce entered, and the prizes won, at a horticultural exhibition held in North Lodge Park.

THE CUT WAS DUG in 1840 by the Great North of England Railway Company, with financial assistance from the town, to take the roads to Yarm and Neasham under the railway tracks. A Bank Top farmer sued the railway company because the previously level access to his land had been lowered by $17\frac{1}{2}$ ft. A road 'accommodation' bridge was built alongside the two railway bridges to restore the farmer's level access from one side to the other. On the left of this photograph is the coal depôt on Hermitage Hill.

THE WIDTH OF 'THE CUT' was increased from 34 ft to 70 ft in 1931. Two new railway bridges were constructed and the road bridge, built for farmer Thomas Baister in the 1840s, was demolished. The work was funded jointly by the London and North Eastern Railway Company and Darlington Corporation, the latter placing the town's coat of arms on each of the outer columns of both bridges to emphasize its financial contribution.

A PLATFORM OF BANK TOP STATION can just be seen at the top of this photograph, taken from the tower of St John's Church. The street running parallel to the station is Adelaide Street, named in honour of the widow of King William IV. Other streets in the area have similar 'royal' connections: Victoria Street, Albert Street and Princes Street.

Left.

AS A RESULT OF ITS SITUATION, the church of St John the Evangelist is one of the most striking buildings in Darlington. Building commenced in 1847, the foundation stone being laid by the 'Railway King', George Hudson. Unfortunately, this stone cannot now be traced. It may be that the stone was subsequently removed, turned, or the inscription erased as a result of Hudson's fall from grace, on account of his dubious financial dealings.

THIS PICTURE OF THE CLEANING STAFF of the North Eastern Railway's Motive Power Depôt (engine shed) at Darlington was taken c. 1910. Engine cleaners had the filthy tasks of clearing the smoke-box in the front of the locomotive and removing the ashes and clinker from the sunken pits both outside and inside the shed. The depôt occupied some acres of land north-east of the station and road access was via Green Street, off Yarm Road.

THE LICENSEE OF THE HOPE INN, Yarm Road, Thomas Collett and his family pose in the early 1920s in front of the public house, between two drays, one horse-drawn and the other a 'modern' motor vehicle. When Thomas died in 1924, his wife Clara took over the licence. The origin of the name of the inn is obscure, but the modern (1976) sign shows the three Gloster Gladiator planes used in the defence of Malta, named Faith, Hope and Charity.

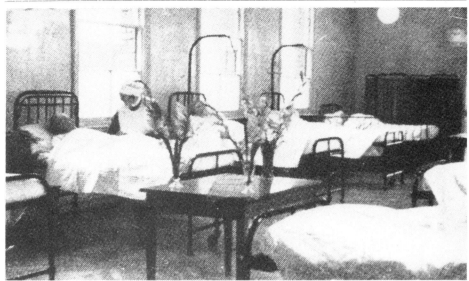

THE DARLINGTON UNION WORKHOUSE moved from the Leadyard in 1868 to a new building in Yarm Road, officially named the New Feethams Institute. In the late 1930s, in one of its changes of name, it became the Darlington Municipal Institution, when it was administered by the Public Assistance section of the Corporation. This picture shows a new female ward which was opened at that time.

CURLING HAS LONG BEEN REGARDED as a sport played only in Scotland, but there were many enthusiasts for the game in Darlington which was played on the Tees (when frozen) and on two ponds. One, Pease's Pond, was part of the Pierremont grounds, but the principal curling pond was at Eastbourne, reached by a lane from Hundens Lane. The clubroom of one of the curling clubs was in the Fleece Hotel in Blackwellgate, the principal patron being Edmund Backhouse. The club was disbanded in the late 1920s.

High Row, Prebend Row, Priestgate and Haughton Road

WHEN THE GENERAL POST OFFICE first permitted the mailing of picture postcards in Britain in 1894, many publishers employed photographers to record the street scenes of towns and cities. Some of the results left much to be desired, as can be seen from this postcard (c. 1910) which prominently features a pair of step-ladders. In a later version of the same card, the publisher painted out the ladders and 'added' more pedestrians.

High Row, Darlington.

CLOSER STUDY OF THIS 'familiar' view of Darlington reveals that the town clock appears to stand at the corner of Priestgate. The printer, who presumably did not know the town, must have reversed the photograph. No publisher's or printer's names appear on the reverse of the card.

SIDGWICK THE DRAPER occupied the two shops on High Row south of the entrance to Mechanics Yard, c. 1895. The small shop between the yard and James Dickson, licensed grocer, was run as a 'Fancy Repository' by Mary Tarn. The general drapers, Ellison and Company, must surely have paid for the privilege and luxury of four gas lamps outside their premises, which would have attracted custom on dark evenings.

The Oldest Pharmacy in Darlington.

ESTABLISHED OVER A CENTURY.

ALWAYS REPUTED FOR THE FINE QUALITY OF DRUGS, TOILET REQUISITES, Etc., BATH AND TOILET SPONGES ESPECIALLY.

Special Attention.

Is drawn to the Optical Department which has recently been fitted with the most modern and approved apparatus by which the smallest Eye defects can be detected.

Careful Attention.

We test each Customer's Eyes carefully, and if we find spectacles are not necessary we do not recommend them, and should the condition of the Eyes show signs of Pathological Disorder, we can discover it and advise our Customer's to consult an Oculist.

Ultimate Benefit.

Clients are assured of good service and ultimate benefit by acting upon the advice we give, whether spectacles are supplied or otherwise.

I. Edward Hodgson J. SWENDEN,

Pharmaceutical Chemist and Optician,

4. HIGH ROW, DARLINGTON.

THIS ADVERTISEMENT (illustrated with a drawing of the rain hopperhead which can still be seen) for J.E. Hodgson's chemist shop No. 14 (not 4) High Row places greater emphasis on its optical department than on the variety of remedies which were stocked. Before J.E. Hodgson acquired the 'oldest pharmacy in Darlington' in 1903–4, it had been run briefly by A. Harburn, who had taken over from J. Swenden in 1901.

Allison & Co.,

20, High Row,
DARLINGTON.

Garden Requisites, Lawn Mowers, Rollers, Chairs and Arches.

Hand-bags, Dress Baskets, Travelling Trunks, in great variety.

ANOTHER EXAMPLE OF THE many small, locally-owned businesses which occupied High Row in the first quarter of the twentieth century, before the town's shopping centre became dominated by branches of national multiple stores.

BINNS OF SUNDERLAND acquired the old-established business of Arthur Saunders (silk mercer) on High Row in 1922. On 24 January 1925, a disastrous fire occurred, and most of the town turned out to watch the flames. As the height of the conflagration coincided with the public houses' closing time, the fire brigade was somewhat hampered by drunks attempting to climb the ladders. The business, which re-opened in August 1925, expanded and gradually took over other shops at the southern end of High Row and in Blackwellgate. The High Row frontage was completed by the acquisition of Sidgwicks in 1935.

THIS VIEW OF THE northern end of High Row, taken in the late 1890s, was used as the front of a card to advertise a shop in Blackwellgate! The two flocks of geese would have been driven (like cattle) into the town to be sold. It was common practice to dip the feet of geese into tar to provide a protective 'sole' for the long walk. At the bottom left can be seen the advertising boards on the side of one of the horse-drawn trams. The shops on High Row include: J. & T. Bayliff (boot maker), M. Tarelli (hardware), R.H. Hall (grocer), W. Dresser (printer), J. Lamont (tailor), J. Dresser (cooper) and the Parisian Mantle Company (draper).

OVER THE CENTURIES, High Row must have staged many assemblies and parades. Here is one of the frequent calls for volunteers to the colours in the First World War. Saxone, shoe retailers, arrived on High Row early in 1916, next to A.A. Atkinson & Co., hatters.

W. DRESSER & SON was an old-established firm on High Row. In 1943 the name was changed to Dressers (Stationers) Ltd. and in 1966 the firm moved a few doors south to its present premises, which had formerly belonged to R. Luck & Sons. The former Dressers shop, (shown here in 1966) was demolished with adjoining premises, and the site is now occupied by the Northern Gas Board and the Abbey National Building Society.

THE HAZARDS FACED by people waiting for buses in the town centre in the early 1950s can be clearly seen in this photograph. Cyclists had to contend with traffic turning both right and left from High Row. Although the trolley-bus wires were still in place, 'trackless trams' were gradually being replaced by a fleet of diesel buses.

THIS AND THE TWO FOLLOWING photographs show some of the changes which have taken place at the Prospect Place/High Row/Northgate corner. In the late 1940s, the plinth of the statue of Joseph Pease was flanked by tulips and provided a convenient site for a road salt-box. Trolley-bus poles and wires abounded, and the taxi awaiting custom from the King's Head occupied the same stand as the horse-drawn cabs had done at the turn of the century.

ALL TROLLEY-BUS WIRES had been removed by 1957, and a forlorn Joseph Pease had become the pivot for what appears to be an unusual, not to say disconcerting, traffic system.

LONG CONSIDERED TO BE A HAZARD, the statue of Joseph Pease was dismantled in June 1958, as part of a new traffic system which included the installation of traffic lights, the moving of the Bondgate pedestrian-crossing and the laying of pavements in front of the bus shelters. By now, many of the original (1901) electric lighting standards had been replaced, but one can still be seen in this photograph to the right of the single-decker bus. Joseph Pease's statue was re-erected on the pavement 20 ft to the south of its original position in September 1958.

PREBEND ROW WAS REGARDED as the main stopping place for both the horse and electric tram service. In this photograph both the Cockerton and Harrowgate Hill horse trams are awaiting departure time. In most pictures of the 1890s, such as this one, very few women are to be seen.

DARLINGTON CORPORATION purchased the horse tram system from the Imperial Tramways Company for £7,000 in January 1902. The intention was to replace the horse trams with a municipally-owned electric tram service, which would serve more parts of the town. During the interim period, the horse trams were leased to C.J. O'Dowd, who is seen here standing in front of double-deck car No. 52. The cars are decorated as part of the town's celebrations of the coronation of King Edward VII in 1902.

'EXCLUSIVE FACTORY TO WEARER FOOTWEAR' proclaimed Freeman, Hardy & Willis Ltd. on Prebend Row. The shop occupied the same premises from 1902 until 1988, when the site was acquired for the Cornmill shopping development.

THE NORTH STAR, a rival to *The Northern Echo*, was published in Crown Street, Darlington from 1881 to 1924. This picture (c. 1919) shows the paper's publicity tent set up at the Darlington Show. The advertised edition featured the latest report of the 'Mad Mullah's' Islamic holy war in Somaliland which lasted from 1899 to 1920.

PRIESTGATE, c. 1900. The Prebend Row corners were occupied respectively by D. Jordon, family grocer and W. Snaith, butcher. The telegraph poles which can be seen on the right-hand side of Priestgate belonged to the National Telephone Company exchange.

A GROUP PHOTOGRAPH of the Darlington postmen, taken in 1900 in the yard to the rear of the post office building in Northgate. At that time the post office provided four deliveries a day in the town, including one at 7.30 p.m.

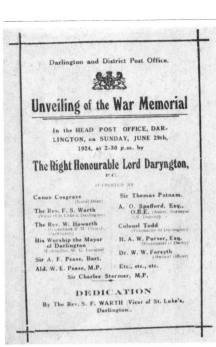

Darlington and District Post Office.

Unveiling of the War Memorial

In the HEAD POST OFFICE, DAR-
LINGTON, on SUNDAY, JUNE 29th,
1924, at 2-30 p.m. by

The Right Honourable Lord Daryngton,
P.C.

SUPPORTED BY

Canon Cosgrave (Rural Dean)	Sir Thomas Putnam.
The Rev. F. S. Warth (Vicar of St. Luke's, Darlington)	A. O. Spafford, Esq., O.B.E. (Asst. Surveyor S. District)
The Rev. W. Howarth (Congreg'l M. Church, Darlington)	Colonel Todd (Postmaster of Darlington)
His Worship the Mayor of Darlington (Councillor W. G. Lonsdale)	H. A. W. Purser, Esq. (Postmaster of Derby)
Sir A. F. Pease, Bart.	Dr. W. W. Forsyth (Medical Officer)
Ald. W. E. Pease, M.P.	Etc., etc., etc.
Sir Charles Starmer, M.P.	

DEDICATION

By The Rev. S. F. WARTH (Vicar of St. Luke's, Darlington).

BARON DARYNGTON OF WITLEY in the County of Surrey, who had been Assistant Postmaster-General from 1915 to 1923, unveiled the Post Office War Memorial plaque in June 1924. Lord Daryngton was no stranger to Darlington. Before being raised to the peerage in 1923, Herbert Pike Pease had served as the town's MP for twenty-five years, apart from one brief spell of ten months. The son of Arthur Pease (1837–98), he was born at Hummersknott in 1867 and died in 1949.

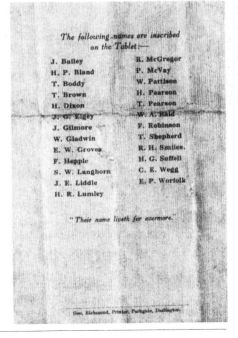

The following names are inscribed on the Tablet :—

J. Bailey	R. McGregor
H. P. Bland	P. McVay
T. Boddy	W. Pattison
T. Brown	H. Pearson
H. Dixon	T. Pearson
J. G. Elgey	W. A. Reid
J. Gilmore	F. Robinson
W. Gladwin	T. Shepherd
E. W. Groves	R. H. Smiles.
F. Hepple	H. G. Suffell
S. W. Langhorn	C. E. Wegg
J. R. Liddle	E. P. Worfolk
H. R. Lumley	

"Their name liveth for evermore."

Geo. Richmond, Printer, Parkgate, Darlington.

OUT OF A TOTAL of 119 post office employees who served, twenty-five gave their lives in the First World War and their names were printed on the reverse of the programme for the unveiling ceremony. When the Northgate post office closed, the plaque was transferred to the Royal Mail sorting office, St Cuthbert's Way.

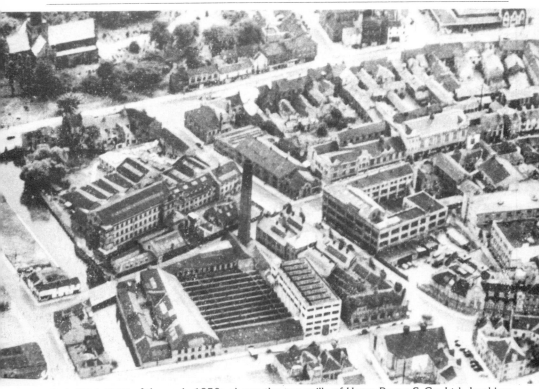

THIS AERIAL SHOT of the early 1950s shows the two mills of Henry Pease & Co. Ltd., backing on to the Skerne and separated by the eastern end of Priestgate. The site of the older mill is now occupied by a car park. The East Street mill was demolished to make way for an indoor ten-pin bowling alley (one of the crazes of the 1960s) which, in turn, has been adapted to accommodate a night club and a multiple furniture store.

ANOTHER AERIAL VIEW of Pease's Mills and Crown Street. The houses which once stood between the River Skerne and Parkgate (formerly Clay Row) are in the process of being demolished to make way for part of the ring road, St Cuthbert's Way. All the raw wool in the warehouse, behind the library, was destroyed by fire in July 1933. The last remaining part of the mills, the chimney, was pulled down in June 1984.

THE PEASE FAMILY WOOLLEN FIRM was founded in 1752 and operated mills on two sites, Priestgate and Leadyard. The latter was destroyed by fire in 1817. In 1837, the company built a mill on the east side of Northgate, in close proximity to the Stockton and Darlington railway line. This mill continued in operation until 1891. The Priestgate mill, seen here, was seriously damaged by fire in February 1894, resulting in over 400 people being thrown out of work, despite the company's efforts to accommodate as many as possible in other departments. The mill, which was rebuilt, finally closed in 1972.

A SECTION OF THE spinning department of Pease's Priestgate Mill.

NEWSPAPERS, LONG REGARDED by successive British governments as channels of subversion, suffered from the imposition of a stamp tax from 1713 to 1855. The repeal of the tax reduced the price of the papers and widened their potential readership. Daily newspapers, priced at one penny, appeared, but Darlington's *The Northern Echo* holds the distinction of being the country's first halfpenny morning daily. The first edition, printed in Penny Yard, was published on 1 January 1870. The *Echo* moved to premises on the north side of Priestgate, before erecting its present building on the corner of Priestgate and Crown Street in 1915.

NEW OFFICES FOR THE BOARD OF GUARDIANS, who administered the Poor Law, were erected on the corner of East Street and Poplar Road in 1896. The architect, George Gordon Hoskins, took pains to make the design blend with that of the Edward Pease Library, which he had also designed. The centrally-heated building contained a 'well-ventilated' waiting room for applicants which was approached from a rear entrance. The Clerk to the Guardians was also the Registrar, and this building continued in use as the Registration Office for births, marriages and deaths until 1973, when the Houndgate Registry Office was opened.

DARLINGTON WAS SLOW TO PROVIDE a municipal electricity service, mainly because the town's gas supply was efficient and relatively cheap. At a champagne reception in December 1900, the Corporation's generators were switched on in time to provide some shops with electric illumination for Christmas. From March 1901, gas street lamps were gradually replaced by electric lighting. By the end of the 1930s, a new plant was required and the building of a power station extension with three chimneys and three cooling towers was commenced in 1939. In 1948, the municipal undertaking was nationalized and the town's power station eventually became a standby for peak capacity periods. It was demolished at the end of 1978.

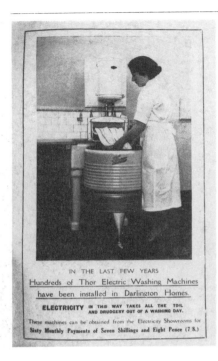

IN THE LAST FEW YEARS
Hundreds of Thor Electric Washing Machines
have been installed in Darlington Homes.

ELECTRICITY IN THIS WAY TAKES ALL THE TOIL AND DRUDGERY OUT OF A WASHING DAY.

These machines can be obtained from the Electricity Showrooms for
Sixty Monthly Payments of Seven Shillings and Eight Pence (7 8.)

BOTH COMMERCIAL AND DOMESTIC USERS benefitted from the Corporation's cheap and efficient electricity supply. Between 1902 and 1928, the electricity undertaking returned £52,000 to the town for rate relief. The town also promoted its inexpensive, clean fuel in its efforts to attract new industry.

THIS GENTLEMAN was one of the Darlington Corporation's Water Department Inspectors. In 1849, a private company supplied piped water from the River Tees at the (now restored) Tees Cottage pumping station. In 1854, the Darlington Board of Health (the predecessor to the council) purchased the company, a transaction which gave the shareholders 100 per cent profit on their original investment. Water was pumped to a reservoir at Bushel Hill (now part of the Mowden housing estate) to provide an adequate pressure for the town's supply. The inhabitants of Harrowgate Hill had to wait until 1872 for a reservoir to provide them with piped water.

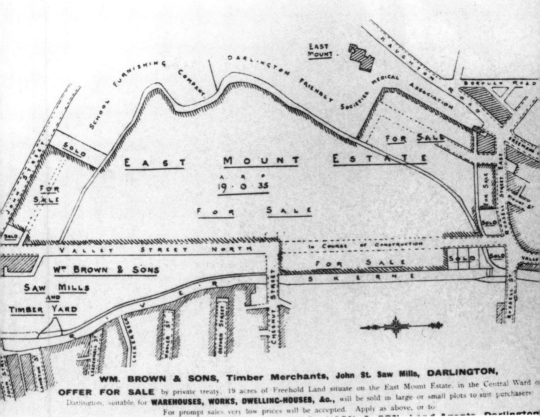

THIS MAP SHOWS the remains of the East Mount estate which was offered for sale in 1906. East Mount, the home of John Pease, was built in 1832 and demolished in the 1960s. The old course of the Skerne can be seen, running parallel to Upper John Street (now East Mount Road) before turning south-west to skirt the base of the hill on which East Mount stood, and rejoining the canalized main stream just north of the Russell Street bridge.

THE PASSING OF THE 1870 Education Act meant that both the money and the site intended for the building of a Catholic church in the Albert Hill area had to be used for the building of a new Catholic school. Opened in 1871, the school of St William, at the corner of Nestfield Street and Barton Street, also served as a church, the altar being partitioned off when not in use. At the beginning of the twentieth century, the building was deemed to be not up to the new standards set for schools and, again, money and a site in Barton Street intended for a church had to be diverted to provide a new school.

Haughton-le-Skerne Area

THE RIVER SKERNE frequently overflowed its banks and flooded low-lying parts of the adjoining area, as is shown in this photograph of Haughton Road. The floods were never so deep as to make the roads impassable to motor vehicles but were more than a nuisance to householders of nearby properties.

HAUGHTON-LE-SKERNE CHURCH.

PICTURE POSTCARDS were often used by shopkeepers as a means of publicity, although the view depicted did not necessarily relate to the location of the shop. Here, the reverse of a view of Haughton Church has been used to advertise Coopers of Parkgate and Gladstone Street. The church of St Andrew, Haughton, was built c. 1125, and the tower added some fifty years later. The church has the distinction of possessing one of the few remaining memorial brasses in the county.

POST CARD.

½d. Stamp
Inland.

THIS SPACE MAY BE USED FOR COMMUNICATION
AS WELL AS THE BACK

FOR ADDRESS ONLY

1d. Stamp
Foreign.

What is the longest word in the language? *SMILES, because there is a mile between the first and last letter.*

YOU WILL BE ALL SMILES *if you buy your Xmas Fruits at COOPER'S, the reason is they are such Excellent Value.*

36, PARKGATE & GLADSTONE ST.,
DARLINGTON.

CANON SHADDICK watches the distribution of Advent Buns which took place on the first Sunday of Advent each year in St Andrew's Church, Haughton. The fine seventeenth-century 'poppy-heads' at the end of each pew can be clearly seen in this early 1940s photograph.

THE MEDIEVAL PART of the rectory at Haughton-le-Skerne can lay claim to being the oldest domestic building in the present Borough of Darlington. In this photograph, the two daughters of the Revd John Charles Fellowes, Rector of Haughton 1903–23, are standing in front of the dorway to what is now Butler House, the rectory having since been divided into two separate residences.

HAUGHTON WAR MEMORIAL stands at the junction of Haughton Road and Salters Lane South.

THE NORTH SIDE of Haughton Green is virtually the same today as it was in the 1890s, when this photograph of Whitehall, Sundial Cottage, 9 The Green and Haughton Villa was taken.

THE NAME OF THE VILLAGE is derived from the Old English 'tun' (homestead or village) and 'halh' (low-lying land near a river). The later addition of 'le-Skerne' was to distinguish the settlement from other Haughtons and Houghtons in the north. The village (unlike Cockerton and Blackwell) has always been a distinct parish from Darlington and was a separate administration unit until incorporated within the town boundaries in 1930.

HAUGHTON HALL, a large, stuccoed eighteenth-century building on the south side of Haughton Green, had extensive grounds which contained a vinery, fernhouses and gardeners' and grooms' cottages. It has had many owners, one being Joseph Porter who was a heckle-maker. The Darlington-born artist, William Bewick (d. 1866) retired to Haughton Hall after a successful career in London, Edinburgh and Dublin. The last owners, Messrs. Paton and Baldwin, sold the hall to Darlington Corporation who converted it into an old people's hostel in 1953. It was sold again in 1980 and reconstructed into three houses in 1981.

STOCKTON ROAD, HAUGHTON-LE-SKERNE.

HAUGHTON'S WOMEN'S INSTITUTE HALL was opened in 1926. It remained the property of the WI until 1986, when it was converted into a nursing home for the elderly.

RED HALL, which stood on the Darlington side of Haughton Bridge, near the northern end of McMullen Road, was built in 1830. There is no recorded reason for the name of the house, but there was fine clay on the estate from which red bricks were made. The twenty-five acre estate was bought in 1965 for housing and the house gave the name to the new estate. There is a tradition of an ancient 'great battle' fought near Red Hall.

Northgate, High Northgate and North Road

Sun Inn, Darlington

THE SUN INN, one of the ancient hostelries of the town, was situated at the corner of Northgate and Prospect Place (which in the seventeenth century was called Sun Row). The inn's 'Long Room', the town's largest meeting room until the building of the Central Hall in 1847, was used for plays, lectures, banquets, religious meetings and musical concerts. The inn was demolished in the 1860s to make way for an extension to the adjacent bank and to enable the entrance to Northgate to be widened.

THIS POSTCARD VIEW of Prospect Place (c. 1910) shows the Victorian extension to the York City and County Bank which was built on the site of the Sun Inn. Although the entrance to Northgate had been widened, it was still not broad enough to allow two electric trams to pass each other.

WHEN THE TWO BUILDINGS of the York City and County Bank were demolished in the early 1920s to make way for the new Midland Bank, the opportunity was again taken to further widen the entrance to Northgate.

THIS BUILDING ON PREBEND ROW, which once stood next to the King's Head, had Dutch-style stepped gables on both the front and side. A hotel in the 1840s, it also served as the parcels' office for two railway companies, the Great North of England (to York) and the Newcastle and Darlington Junction (to Newcastle). One of the eighty public houses and beer retailers in the centre of Darlington in the 1850s, it became successively Pomfret's Hotel, the Commercial Inn and the Borough Inn (later Hotel). After losing its licence in 1909, it ended its days as Monument Chambers, part of which was occupied by the Beadell School of Dancing in the 1950s.

LOCAL PHOTOGRAPHER S.H. Wood's view of High Row shows the Northgate entrance to the King's Head Hotel with its canopy extending to the edge of the pavement to ensure that guests were not exposed to the elements.

THE LINE OF HORSE CABS, awaiting fares from the King's Head, seems to be dangerously close to the tram tracks. The hotel, which was opened in June 1893, was built to replace a seventeenth-century coaching inn which had stood on the same site. At the turn of the century, the shops incorporated into its frontage were Fenwick's (wines and spirits) the owners of the hotel, J.H. Waites (hosier) and W. Swalwell (fancy repository).

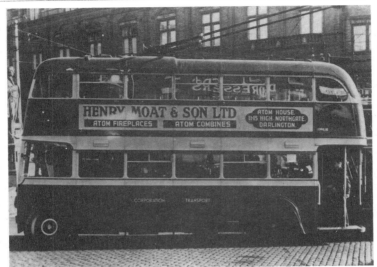

ONE OF THE SIX double-decker trolley buses which were acquired by the town in 1949, negotiating the 'Joseph Pease' corner into Bondgate. After the introduction of diesel buses in November 1951, these 'trackless trams' were sold to Doncaster and eventually ended their working lives in Bradford.

NORTHGATE, LOOKING TOWARDS HIGH ROW. It is difficult to believe from this photograph that this was once part of the busy Great North Road, although it is obvious that the hazard of parked vehicles is nothing new in Darlington. The buildings on the right-hand side contained (from the left) Lea Bros. (drapers), W. Stanton (bookseller), W. Wallis (tailor), Cox & Falconer (furniture), F. Chilton (tailor), J. Robinson (chemist) and the Three Tuns Inn, licensee John Turnbull.

THE FIRM OF COX & FALCONER occupied the Exchange Buildings in the 1890s, shown clearly on the previous photograph. The business remained in Northgate until 1963, when it moved to Horsemarket to take over the former premises of Lears, hardware and ironmongery.

THE GROCERY FIRM OF DAVID FOX originated on High Row in 1864. In 1889, its Oriental Café was opened in Northgate. The café owed its name to the style of the original decor of its four rooms – Indian, Arabian, Moorish and Japanese. This 1930s advertisement shows a later 'Olde England' room. The café moved to Bondgate in 1939, closing in 1958.

THE CONGREGATIONAL BICENTENARY MEMORIAL CHURCH in Union Street opened in 1862 and was designed by the Darlington architect, J.P. Pritchett. The church replaced the small chapel in the Leadyard and was one of the 100 built by the Congregational Union to commemmorate the 200th anniversary of the passing of the 1662 Act of Uniformity. This Act deprived dissenting clergy of their livings and created the breach between the established church and the non-conformists.

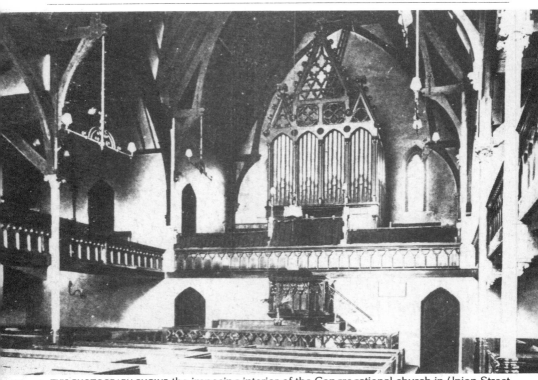

THIS PHOTOGRAPH SHOWS the imposing interior of the Congregational church in Union Street which became redundant in 1972 after the merger with the English Presbyterian church. The building, although now used as a carpet shop and warehouse, has suffered little interior alteration.

NORTHGATE ON A GREY WINTER DAY, C. 1890. The rebuilding of the King's Head (architect, George Gordon Hoskins) had reached roof level. Between the Bay Horse Hotel (third building from the right) and Crown Street, the single tram track widens to a passing loop.

THIS IS VIRTUALLY THE SAME NORTHGATE SCENE, photographed a few weeks later after a moderately heavy fall of snow, the cleared tramway route being used by all the (horse-drawn) traffic. The pedimented building, in the right-hand middle distance, contained the offices of the North Eastern Railway, and had formerly been the headquarters of the Stockton and Darlington Railway Company. During the First World War, this building became a troop canteen and in 1919 was converted to accommodate the Queen's Hall and shops. The site is now occupied by a branch of Boots the Chemists.

THE SOUTHERN END OF NORTHGATE has been altered out of all recognition during the course of the twentieth century. Looking northwards (c. 1905), compare the rebuilt Bay Horse Hotel on the corner of Commercial Street with its modest predecessor, which can be seen in the photograph on p. 93.

Northgate, Darlington.

THE PRUDENTIAL ASSURANCE COMPANY built new offices at the north-west corner of Northgate and Commercial Street in 1911, opposite to the Bay Horse Hotel. A statue of Prudentia was placed in a large niche over the front door. When this part of Northgate was 'developed' in the 1960s, the statue was removed and is now in the North Road Railway Museum.

THIS POSTCARD WAS COMMISSIONED by G.W. Fearnley, stationer and tobacconist of No. 73 Bondgate. The printer's erroneous 'North Gate' might give the impression that Darlington was once a walled town, but the suffix 'gate' in the names of the town's ancient thoroughfares is derived from the old Norse word for 'street'. Next door to Haward & Sons, house furnishers, was the town's branch of F.W. Woolworth, which opened in 1913.

THE SITE OF THE NORTHGATE TOBACCONIST, John Sinclair Ltd., now lies under the ring road roundabout. Continuing southwards along Northgate were: W. Barratt (boots and shoes), Home and Colonial Stores (grocers) and Bramwell and Harbron (jewellers) who, as the sign above the shop states, celebrated its diamond jubilee in the year of the photograph, 1935.

THIS PHOTOGRAPH of 1969 shows the splendid bay windows of Nos. 66 and 68 Northgate, sandwiched between British Home Stores and Marks and Spencer Ltd. A butcher's shop at the turn of the century, it had been the home of F.W. Woolworth for many years before that company's move to larger premises. Its last tenant, before demolition to make way for a branch of Mothercare, was Jay's, a house furnishing business.

THIS POSTCARD VIEW shows the lake and boat house of North Lodge Park, c. 1905. North Lodge (for many years the Council's Education offices and now a Teachers' Centre) had been built in 1838 for John Beaumont Pease, and was purchased by the Corporation in 1901, the grounds being opened as a public park two years later. The lake was not intended for public boating, being merely a decorative feature. In 1932, it was drained and the site landscaped.

THE RESIDENTS OF SELBOURNE TERRACE, off Gladstone Street, decorated their houses and provided a children's tea party to celebrate the signing of the Armistice in 1918.

THIS PHOTOGRAPH OF NORTHGATE was taken c. 1900. Two of the town's music shops can be seen, Archibald Ramsden Ltd. and (next door to St George's Church) James Hoggett's, founded by a member of a Darlington family long associated with music. The gabled eighteenth-century house, between Ramsden's and the Salvation Army Citadel, was at this time the Arthur Pease Memorial Home for the Queen's Nurses. Maintained by voluntary subscriptions and donations, these nurses cared for the sick poor in their own homes until the advent of the National Health Service.

THE WHITE-BEARDED GENTLEMAN is John Wharton, whose ironmongery shop was situated next to the police station in Northgate. Elected to the council in 1874, his campaign posters had declared that he would not canvass for votes. He also promised to fight to obtain all-day Sunday access to South Park, which up to then had remained closed on Sunday mornings to allow the park keeper to attend church. Another cause dear to Wharton's heart was the retention of privies and ash pits which he considered to be more beneficial than water closets. He died in 1897, aged seventy-two.

ST GEORGE'S PRESBYTERIAN CHURCH (since 1972 the United Reformed Church) was opened in March 1869. Built on land purchased from John Pease, the church was designed by local architects, John Ross and Robert Lamb. Good use was made of the sloping site with meeting rooms accommodated under the east end of the church. The 120 ft spire had to be repaired after suffering storm damage in 1903.

BUILT ON THE SITE of a former Baptist chapel in Leadenhall Street in 1883 to the design of J.P. Pritchett, St Luke's Parish Church had become too small for its congregation by the turn of the century. In 1910, an appeal for funds was launched, targetted particularly at railway shareholders and workers. In February 1917, the new St Luke's Church in Corporation Road was opened, a carved stone plaque on the exterior of its west wall proclaiming it to be the 'Railway Pioneers Memorial Church'. The old church in Leadenhall Street was used for a variety of purposes, including a Labour Exchange, Army Recruiting Office and a warehouse before its demolition in 1978.

THE POLICE STATION in Northgate at the corner of Chesnut Street was built in 1867 to replace the small and inconveniently-situated station in Grange Road. The new station was described as having 'suitable rooms for the magistrates, dwellings for the constables and cells for the prisoners'.

THE NEWLY-DELIVERED ELECTRIC TRAM No. 16 on display in June 1904. The main route ran from Harrowgate Hill to Eastbourne, with a cross-over between the 'up' and 'down' tracks near Leadenhall Street. Despite the 'evidence' of the tram's destination blind, the proposed evening service between the town centre and the Theatre Royal (now the Cannon Cinema) for which the cross-over had been constructed, was never put into operation.

ONE OF A SERIES OF POSTCARDS issued after the Darlington Lifeboat Saturday of 1900. The procession, in which all the societies of the town took part, is shown in Corporation Road having just turned out of Northgate.

WHERE COCKER BECK runs beneath the road on its way to join the Skerne marks the division between Northgate and High Northgate. The gradient of the road is clearly shown in this photograph of 1900. The chimney of Pease's Railway Mill (by then disused) can be seen on the right. At the entrance to Leadenhall Street, the metal arch marks the approach to the stables of J.W. Waterson, cab proprietor. T.W. Thorpe, furniture broker, occupied the shop beneath the tower (left foreground).

J.C. YARE RAN AN ANTIQUE GALLERY at the corner of High Northgate and Westbrook in the 1930s, when plus-fours were obviously the fashion for Darlington's 'men-about-town'.

BUILT AT THE NEWCASTLE FORTH STREET WORKS of Robert Stephenson & Company, *Locomotion* was conveyed by horse-drawn cart to Aycliffe Lane (where the present Heighington station now is) and manoeuvred onto the railway line on 10 September 1825. The locomotive worked on the Stockton and Darlington Railway until 1850, when it was acquired by Pease and Partners for use in colliery yards. In 1857, it was 'retired' and placed on this plinth outside North Road station – seen here with the former S & D carriage works in the background.

A MAJOR CONTRIBUTION to the 1925 celebrations of the centenary of the opening of the Stockton and Darlington Railway was a parade of locomotives. Bringing up the rear, the venerable *Locomotion* hauled a small number of wagons which carried members of local theatrical groups, attired in 'period' costume.

THE S & D RAILWAY CENTENARY CELEBRATIONS in 1925, attended by the Duke and Duchess of York (the future King George VI and Queen Elizabeth), extended over three days. At the centenary banquet on the second day and the special luncheon on the third day, both held in a marquee at the newly-built wagon works at Faverdale, the guests were entertained by the Claude Gildersleeve Orchestra. After Army service, Claude Gildersleeve had settled in Darlington and found work as a piano tuner and repairer for Archibald Ramsden, before becoming well-known as a musician and composer. He died in 1956, aged seventy-seven.

ALTHOUGH THE NORTH ROAD STATION of 1842 is not actually in North Road, it stands close to the site of the original level crossing which carried the S & D Railway line across the Great North Road. When the decision was taken to replace the inconvenient crossing with a bridge in 1856, the line of the old road was moved slightly to the east and its level lowered to pass under the bridge.

BOROUGH OF DARLINGTO

THE RAILWAY JUBILEE.

A REQUISITION, signed by 102 Tradesmen, having been presented to me, ask
to take such measures as I think fit to secure a

"GENERAL HOLIDA

From Two o'clock, on MONDAY AFTERNOON, September 27th, to WEDNE
MORNING, September 29th; and a further Requisition from the Owners of Iron
in the Borough, having also been sent to me, stating that a "General Holid
TUESDAY will necessitate the closing of their Works, inasmuch as it will incl
places of business, and objecting thereto, I therefore recommend that the

SHOPS

In the Town be CLOSED on MONDAY, the 27th, from Two in the Afternoo
WEDNESDAY MORNING, the 29th instant.

H. FELL PEAS

Darlington, 16th September, 1875.

MAYOR

WILLIAM DRESSER, GAS-PRINTING WORKS, 41, HIGH ROW, DARLINGTON.

THE MAYOR OF DARLINGTON, Henry Fell Pease of Brinkburn, issued this notice on 16 September 1875 in the run-up to the celebration of the 50th anniversary of the opening of the Stockton and Darlington Railway. The highlight of the ceremonies was to be the unveiling of the statue of Joseph Pease on High Row on the afternoon of Tuesday, 28 September.

THE SHILDON WORKS COMPANY, a wholly-owned subsidiary of the S & D Railway Company, had been set up to manufacture locomotives at Shildon. In 1859, the decision was taken to move the work to Darlington, and North Road Locomotive Works were opened on 1 January 1863. In July of that year, the S & D (and its subsidiary the Shildon Works Co) was amalgamated with the North Eastern Railway Company. Here is a group photograph of the Works Manager of North Road and his foremen (date unknown). The Works, for over a century one of the town's major places of employment, closed on 1 April 1966.

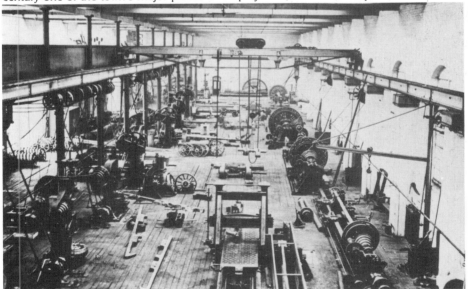

THE NORTH ROAD WORKS, which in its heyday, employed over 2,200 workers, occupied an area bounded by North Road, Denmark and Westmoreland Streets and Whessoe Road. Its North Road frontage from the Railway Institute to the Works Manager's office was over 230 yds long. There were many large individual workshops, some of which were over 150 yds long, such as the frame shop.

THE NORTH EASTERN RAILWAY COMPANY was a paternalistic employer and encouraged its staff to participate in social activities by providing facilities. The company supplied the instruments for its Darlington Brass Band, seen here at North Road Works in 1913.

DARLINGTON'S REPUTATION as a 'railway' town rested not only on the large number of railway employees in the town, but also on associated industries which manufactured equipment for railway companies. One such firm was William Kitching's foundry in Tubwell Row which had opened in 1791 and produced work for the S & D Railway from 1824. In the 1830s, the firm moved to Hopetown and became the nucleus for what is now Whessoe Ltd. In this 1890 photograph, the men of Kitching's Foundry are taking a welcome break from their heavy labours.

ANOTHER LARGE EMPLOYER in Darlington was the Darlington Forge Ltd. which was first established at Albert Hill in 1845 and later took over the Darlington Iron Company and the South Durham Iron Works Company. The Putnam family was long associated with the firm and Thomas Putnam, who became managing director in 1897, was knighted in 1918. These photographs formed part of a brochure issued in 1914 on the occasion of a visit by 300 members of the Institute of Naval Architects. The Forge closed in 1963.

ALTHOUGH DARLINGTON FORGE did supply railway products (including the first rails for Japan), it was renowned for the huge castings, up to 100 tons in weight, produced for shipbuilding and ship repair. The firm provided castings for the *Queen Mary* and many Cunard liners, including the *Mauretania* and the *Lusitania* of First World War fame. This is a photograph of one of these (stern frame) castings. The 12-ton steam hammer once used at the Forge is now in the Beamish Museum.

Gas Department

DARLINGTON CORPORATION was justly proud of the reasonably-priced gas which was supplied by the municipal gas works. Two-thirds of consumers in the town (about 18,000 people), paid for their gas by 'penny in the slot' meters which were emptied seven or eight times a year. In this 1937 photograph, the Gas Department puts its motor fleet on display.

ON THE LAST DAY of the service in August 1903, a decorated double-decker horse tram waits at the terminus at Wales Street, North Road before returning to the town centre. In the background, the building with the bell cote was St Paul's school, which was built in 1863 and closed in the late 1920s.

BUILT ON A SITE provided by William Barningham, owner of one of the town's ironworks, North Road Methodist Church was opened in 1872 to replace an 1863 chapel in Denmark Street. In 1885 the North Road Church became the head of the newly-formed North Circuit in the town. In 1965 the church was demolished and the Northland Methodist Church was erected in its place, opening in January 1967.

RATHER THAN RELYING TOTALLY on the town's fire brigade, many of the larger companies in Darlington had private fire appliances which could be manned by their own employees. Here is the shining new fire engine of Robert Stephenson and Company of Springfield Works in 1914.

THE FIRM OF ROBERT STEPHENSON AND COMPANY was founded in Newcastle by George Stephenson, his son Robert, Edward Pease and Michael Longridge of Bedlington in 1823. The company built *Locomotion* in 1825 for the S & D Railway and, fifteen locomotives later, produced the famous *Rocket* for the Liverpool and Manchester Railway. In 1930, 'Stevvies' produced a replica of *Rocket* (seen here outside the Springfield Works) for the centenary celebrations of the L & M Railway Company.

AS THE BUSINESS EXPANDED, Stephenson's found the Newcastle site to be too small to cope with the inflow of work. In 1901 the firm moved to Darlington, the first new locomotive being produced there the following year. Railway engines were exported to many countries, including this splendid example for the South African Railway in 1935. In 1937, the company amalgamated with the Newcastle firm of R. & W. Hawthorn (established 1817) to become Stephenson and Hawthorn. The Springfield Works closed in 1964.

ONE OF THE MANY small laundry and dry cleaning businesses which once served the housewives of Darlington.

Blackwellgate, Grange Road, Coniscliffe Road and Duke Street

THE COUNTY HOTEL in 1896, when Robert Flint was the landlord. The original name of the inn on the corner of Blackwellgate and Grange Road was the Black Bull, which is reputed to have been the model for The Black Bear in R.L. Stevenson's novel *Rob Roy*. In 1956 the building was demolished as part of a road-widening scheme and a new County Hotel was erected in the space of ninety working days.

THE BUILDINGS AND BUSINESSES which once stood at the corner of Blackwellgate and Skinnergate were very modest. They included: B. Stockton (newsagent), R.H. Pomfret (dyer) and R.W. Drewery (grocer).

BLACKWELLGATE WAS REPORTED to have 'divers houses of evill note' in 1614, but respectability reigns in this photograph of 1910. One of the town's elegant electric lamp standards graces the street. Each town centre public house acted as an unofficial office for local carriers. From the Three Blue Bells Inn on Mondays (market days), goods could be sent to Croft, Dalton and Great Smeaton at 3 p.m. and to Stapleton, Barton and Middleton Tyas at 3.30 p.m.

THIS BUILDING ON THE CORNER of Blackwellgate and Houndgate is still recognizable today, even though the ground floor has been altered drastically. Richardson & Co were offering spectacles to the public in 1900 at a cost of 4s. 6d.

BAINBRIDGE BARKER, Darlington's first department store, began as a small shop in Skinner-gate and gradually expanded to occupy the large corner site from the Mechanics Institute to Drewery's the grocers in Blackwellgate. Standing within the 'protection' of his painted circle, the policeman on point duty (whose white raincoat is hung conveniently on the County Hotel) was very necessary at this awkward corner on the A1.

ANOTHER VIEW OF BLACKWELLGATE in the 1930s, showing how narrow this part of the Great North Road was. It had been even narrower before 1833, when Francis Mewburn had campaigned to raise sufficient money to purchase 5 ft of ground opposite to the Fleece Inn to enable the road to be widened.

THE FLEECE HOTEL was another of the ancient inns of Darlington, having been in existence for nearly 300 years when it closed in 1968. One of its landlords, who died in 1739, aged ninety-three, was reputed to have kept the inn since 1688. The site is now occupied by Boyes' department store.

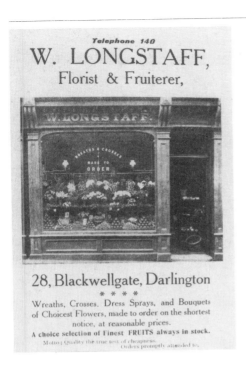

Telephone 140

W. LONGSTAFF,

Florist & Fruiterer,

28, Blackwellgate, Darlington

* * * *

Wreaths, Crosses, Dress Sprays, and Bouquets
of Choicest Flowers, made to order on the shortest
notice, at reasonable prices.

A choice selection of Finest FRUITS always in stock.

Motto: Quality the true test of cheapness.

Orders promptly attended to.

THIS ADVERTISEMENT for W. Longstaff, florist and fruiterer, appeared in a guide to the town in 1900. The site of the shop is now covered by the Royal Bank of Scotland building.

LADY CYCLISTS would find it impossible to gossip in the middle of Blackwellgate today! Next to the County Hotel, George Jobling's garage sign foretells the shape of things to come, when Darlington's main streets would be choked with traffic.

SYDNEY H. WOOD, who died in 1959, set up business in Blackwellgate after serving his apprenticeship with Frank Cooper. He became the official photographer to successive mayors of Darlington. The 'Tudor' façade of his premises, which was demolished in 1953 after being acquired by Binns, was said to attract tourists to his studio, and he photographed many visiting celebrities.

THE 'CARTE-DE-VISITE', a photograph so called because it was printed onto stiff card of a size similar to that of a visiting card, became extremely popular from around 1860. The photographer used the reverse to advertise his services. Ivy House, Bondgate, now lies in the path of the fourth (and last) section of the town's ring road system, and has languished under the threat of demolition for many years.

BORN IN IPSWICH, Stephen Edward Piper (1813–94) served with the Lancers in the Spanish Carlist War and was wounded in 1826. In 1841 he arrived in Darlington to practice medicine and was appointed Medical Officer to the town's Board of Health seven years later. In 1867, he became the MOH to the newly-created Borough of Darlington, a position he held until 1882. It was mainly due to his campaigning and forthright reports that the town acquired a supply of pure drinking water and an adequate sewerage system.

PUNCH BOWL YARD, SKINNERGATE, received special mention in Doctor Piper's annual report of 1850 to the Board of Health. While inveighing against the filthy and overcrowded living conditions in most yards of the town, he reported that 'one of the worst scenes I ever witnessed was in Punch Bowl Yard.' The yard's name came from an inn which once stood in the centre.

JOHN KITCHING (1854–1935), with his wife Annie Elizabeth and their children John, Alfred and Phoebe. John was the son of Alfred Kitching the iron founder, who was the designer and builder of the railway engine, *Derwent*, now in the North Road Railway Museum. The Kitching family lived at Branksome Hall (formerly Westfield Hall) from 1885 until 1948.

THE ORIGINAL TREVELYAN HOTEL was situated at the north-west corner of Skinnergate and Coniscliffe Road. The hotel moved to its new premises on the opposite corner in the late 1870s as a Commercial (and Temperance) establishment. In 1890 the owner, Edward Wooler, persuaded the licensing authorities to transfer the licence of the Hat and Feathers public house in Church Row to the Trevelyan Hotel. He then presented the Hat and Feathers to the Council for demolition as a means of improving the market place and the approach to St Cuthbert's Church.

The——
IMPERIAL HOTEL,
DARLINGTON,

is a superior Hotel, conveniently situated near the centre of the town and within 10 minutes' walk of the Railway Station.

This Hotel is the only "free house" of its class in Darlington, and consequently the comfort of guests is not subordinated to the sale of Liquors. There are no vaults connected with the premises, which insures a degree of privacy and home comfort not often met with in provincial hotels.

Gentlemen will find it greatly to their advantage to make this hotel their head-quarters, and to work the district from Darlington as affording an agreeable change of air from the smoky manufacturing towns of the neighbourhood.

BY THE TURN OF THE CENTURY, the hotel had acquired a grander name and, from the tone of this 1903 advertisement, was hoping to attract a superior type of guest.

WHEN DARLINGTON BOROUGH COUNCIL acquired the old Trevelyan Hotel in 1878 as part of yet another road widening scheme, a condition of sale was that no alcohol should be sold in any new building on the site. In 1897 the imposing, gabled building designed by G.G. Hoskins for the North of England School Furnishing Company was opened.

GRANGE ROAD IN THE GRIP OF WINTER, c. 1900. Unlike much of the rest of the town centre, this part of Grange Road is now, as then, mainly occupied by small, individual businesses. In this photograph can be seen (from the County Hotel): T. Turnbull (cab office), Miss Ellison (fancy draper), Mrs Joynes (dressmaker), H.S. Bonsall (hairdresser), Hoggett & Sons (music and musical instruments) and T. Harrison (upholsterer).

GRANGE ROAD FESTOONED WITH FLAGS and bunting on the occasion of the visit of the Duke and Duchess of York in June 1895. The huge banner proclaims 'We give you a hearty welcome'.

J.J. HOBSON'S extensive furniture showrooms at No. 22 Grange Road in 1920 guaranteed early delivery on every item ordered.

THE CLEVELAND CAR COMPANY opened on the corner of Grange Road and West Street in 1907. This photograph of its eye-catching buildings was used in its early advertising. The site is now occupied by a branch of Comet Discount Stores.

THIS POSTCARD, from a photograph by S.H. Wood, shows (through the trees) Orwell House and the Grange Road Baptist Church. Orwell House, a hotel from 1924, was demolished in 1976 to make way for one lane of the dual carriageway of Victoria Road. The original entrance to the town's famed 'Crocus Walk' can be seen in the centre of the photograph.

DARLINGTON'S ORIGINAL BAPTIST CHAPEL in Archer Street now serves as a Masonic Hall. Because of increasing congregations, a new church, designed by John Green, was built on land in Grange Road acquired from the Duke of Northumberland. The opening services were held in June 1871.

GRANGE ROAD IN THE LATE 1940s. The garage of the Motor Delivery Company occupied a strategic site on the A1.

NEWCOMERS TO DARLINGTON might imagine that this avenue obtained its name from its situation on the south side of the town. The land on which the houses were built formed part of the grounds of Southend, the house of Joseph Pease (now the Grange Hotel). When the estate was sold in 1897, the land was acquired for housing development by the Southend Estate Company, and Southend, Beechwood and Oakdene Avenues were subsequently laid out.

South End Avenue, Darlington

DARLINGTON CORPORATION purchased a strip of land at the Grange Road edge of the Southend estate in 1899 with the restrictive covenant that it 'shall forever hereafter remain unbuilt upon'. Opened to the public in 1901, the area has become known, for obvious reasons, as the 'Crocus Walk'. Despite the covenant, and public indignation, over 20 yds were lost in 1976 to the ring road roundabout. This view is taken from the south before the land purchased by the Southend Estate Company had been developed.

THIS POSTCARD, signed by the teaching staff, was sent to one of the 'old girls' of Polam Hall in July, 1938. 'Polam House' was first rented in 1900 by Miss Bayes, the headmistress of Polam School. Ultimately, nine of these ten houses were to be rented to provide overflow accommodation for the school. After her marriage to Oswald Baynes, Miss Bayes lived in Polam House until her retirement in 1933. Gradually, over the years, the school vacated the houses, Polam House (by then owned by the school) being sold in the 1960s.

IN THE DAYS when postcards provided an inexpensive and swift means of sending messages, itinerant photographers would often produce views of houses for their occupants, printed on postcards. Here are two local examples: (top) Reethville, Langholm Crescent, and (bottom) The Lindens, Coniscliffe Road, from which Linden Avenue's name is derived.

A STREET PARTY for the children of Powlett Street, on the occasion of the Silver Jubilee of King George V in 1935.

CHARLES KNOTT & SON'S premises on the corner of Duke Street and Raby Terrace, photographed in 1960. The business was established in 1876.

Bondgate and Woodland Road

BONDGATE IN 1900. At this time the statue of Joseph Pease was graced by four globe gas lamps. The businesses on Prospect Place included: Jonathan Dresser (hairdresser), George Tanfield (draper), S. Hopper (clocks and watches) and Clarkson and Company (grocers). George Tanfield (d. 1902) built an orphanage in Freeman's Place which was later to become Airedale House, a Salvation Army Hostel.

THIS ADVERTISEMENT in 1912 for J.W. Harrower's establishment at No. 9 Prospect Place displays the latest Darlington fashions.

A WINTRY SCENE IN BONDGATE, c. 1900. The separate manor of Bondgate-in-Darlington is thought to have been created, at the end of the twelfth century, at the same time as the medieval borough of Darlington. Unlike the freemen of the borough, the tenants of Bondgate were required to perform services for their lord, the Bishop of Durham.

A DISPLAY OF CARRIAGES outside the offices of A.E. Middleton, 'proprietor of cabs and dog carts', No. 37 Bondgate (c. 1903). A careful study of the south side of Bondgate reveals that these once-substantial houses still exist behind the later shop fronts.

A PRINT OF BONDGATE from 1850, showing the cottages (demolished in 1854) which once stood in the centre of the street at its widest point.

BONDGATE IN THE 1950s, when it was still relatively safe to stand and talk in the middle of the road and car parking was permitted. The pole in the centre of the street carried the wires for the Cockerton trolley-bus service, and also allowed the buses to make U-turns in Bondgate. The shops on the right-hand side of the picture, at the corner of Archer Street, were eventually to be demolished to make way for the ring road.

THE NARROW ENTRANCE to Bondgate School, where these girls are performing Swedish drill, can be seen in the centre background of this photograph. The lane from Bondgate, now leading to a builder's yard, still exists today. The site of the school yard now forms part of the grounds of British Telecom's exchange.

MRS SHUTT, THE HEADMISTRESS of Bondgate School, photographed with a fellow teacher and senior pupils in 1907. The Bondgate Sunday and Day Schools, opened in January 1858, were financed by money raised by Bondgate Methodist Church. In 1908, the day school was leased to the local Education Authority. It closed in 1937.

THE ORDER OF THE SONS OF TEMPERANCE held its 81st Annual Session in the Co-operative Hall, Priestgate in June 1936. A reception tea, organized by the Darlington Reception Committee (pictured here), was held in Bondgate Memorial Hall.

A VERY EARLY PHOTOGRAPH (1860) of members of the Darlington Quoit Club. Founded in 1846, the club is possibly the oldest in the country. The Local History Library, Crown Street, possesses a framed copy of this photograph, on the back of which are written the following names: Smith, Allison, Hardy, Swinburn, Brady, Preston, Lear jun., Potts, Child, Harrison Lea and Graham.

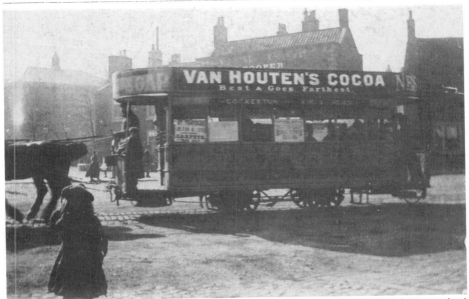

A HORSE TRAM of the Stockton and Darlington Steam Tramway Company, photographed opposite the Salt Yard and the entrance lane to Bondgate School. Although the company operated some steam trams in Stockton, only the horse-drawn variety ran in Darlington. The YMCA, which came to Darlington in the 1870s, occupied Ivy House (the upper story of which can be seen behind the tram), before moving to Granville House, at the corner of Portland Place.

THE WESTERN END OF BONDGATE, c. 1910. This photograph nicely illustrates the limits of the town's electric street lighting. An electric lamp standard can be seen on the corner of Greenbank Road and Bondgate, but the stanchion in the foreground, which carried wires for the electric tram system, bears two gas lamps.

A DARLINGTON HORSE TRAM, decorated to celebrate the coronation of King Edward VII in August 1902. Although the sign above the tram depôt door reads 'Imperial Tramways Co. Ltd.', by this time the system was owned by the Corporation and had been leased to Charles J. O'Dowd (pictured here in the light suit). Darlington's horse tram depôt was situated in Woodland(s) Road. It (and the adjacent Granville House) now forms part of the premises of Messrs. E. Williamson, Motor Dealers.

GREENBANK HOSPITAL, designed by G.G. Hoskins, was built in the grounds of the demolished house, Greenbank. Opened in December 1884, it replaced the town's first small hospital in Russell Street, and was supported by voluntary contributions and donations, plus any fees which patients could afford. Domestic servants, however, were not admitted unless their employers undertook to pay the full cost. Fund raising was always a major problem, but various extensions were built with the aid of generous donations.

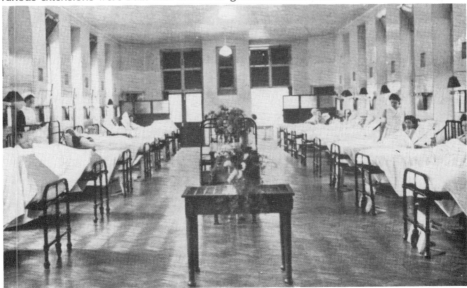

EVEN WHEN THE WAR MEMORIAL HOSPITAL in Hollyhurst Road was opened in 1932, the Greenbank Hospital continued to be used. Again, voluntary contributions supported the provision of hospital services, many of the local workforce agreeing to small deductions being made from their pay. The photograph shows a new female ward in 'the Memorial', which was opened just before the inauguration of the National Health Service.

SWISS COTTAGE, a 'romantic' feature of the grounds of James Backhouse's residence, West Lodge, was built in 1831. Last used to provide staff accommodation for the Memorial Hospital, the Swiss Cottage was demolished in 1974.

BUILT IN THE EARLY 1830s for Robert Botcherby, Pierremont was sometimes known as Botcherby Hall. In 1845, the estate was acquired by Henry Pease the brother of Joseph, who extended the house and developed the gardens. In 1864 he purchased land to the south of Woodland(s) Road to improve the view from his home. Gradually, the boggy ground was transformed into an attractive pleasure garden, open to all. In 1910, the seedsmen, Kent & Brydon, of Tubwell Row, acquired Pierremont South Park as a nursery, but it was eventually to disappear under the houses of the appropriately-named Pierremont Gardens. The large ornamental fountain is now in South Park.

BUILT TO THE DESIGNS OF J.P. PRITCHETT, the British and Foreign Schools Society College for the Training of Mistresses for Elementary Schools was opened in 1875, much of the finance coming from the town's wealthy Quaker families, including the Peases and Backhouses. The two views are in stark contrast, the top showing the newly-completed college in an almost-treeless landscape, the (later) bottom photograph depicting it ivy-clad and surrounded by leafy foliage. Stanhope Green and College Green were two of the names suggested for the proposed open public space to the east of the college. A compromise was reached and Stanhope Green, the landscaping of which had been financed by profits from the Corporation's Gas and Water Department, was opened in 1879. In September 1979, the college became the town's Art Centre.

The Training College, Darlington. – Front.

THE DARLINGTON HIGH SCHOOL FOR GIRLS, financed by voluntary subscriptions, donations and fees, was opened in Trinity Road in 1885. It was controlled by a committee of prominent local residents until 1906, when the Durham County Council assumed responsibility. In 1911, the move to the new purpose-built school in Cleveland Avenue (pictured here) was made. Control of the High School returned to the town when Darlington became a County Borough in 1915. In 1955, the school again moved to new premises at Hummersknott, on the western outskirts of the town. The Cleveland Avenue buildings then formed the nucleus for the College of Technology.

Cockerton

FORCETT STREET, COCKERTON (demolished 1972) was built in the mid-nineteenth century to provide working-class housing for railway and foundry workers.

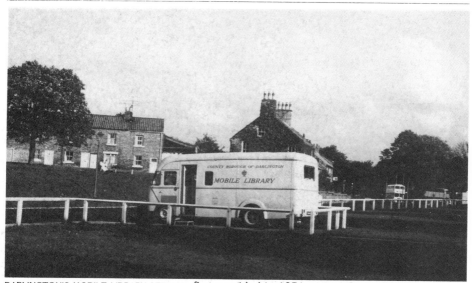

DARLINGTON'S MOBILE LIBRARY SERVICE, first provided in 1951, visited Cockerton Green every Thursday until the purpose-built branch library at the junction of Woodland Road and the Green opened in 1970.

The Fountain, Cockerton

THE CHURCH COMMISSIONERS, the owners of Cockerton Green, leased it to the town for nineteen years in 1923, at a rent of 10 s. (50p) a year. In 1962, the Commissioners freely transferred ownership of the Green to the Corporation, on condition that it should continue to be used as an open space. The fountain which once stood in Stanwick Park, near Richmond, was presented to the village in 1924 by Councillor Sutherland.

COCKERTON'S WEST BRIDGE, C. 1910. Few people realize nowadays that they are crossing over West Beck, now culverted to run under a much-widened Newton Lane.

THE COTTAGES OF SUNNY TERRACE, COCKERTON, some of which were of wooden cruck construction, survived until the 1960s, when they were demolished to make way for a row of modern shop units.

WEST AUCKLAND ROAD formed part of the 'Coal Road', along which carts and pack animals carried coal from the West Auckland mines before the advent of the Stockton and Darlington Railway. The Alma Hotel (now the Brown Trout) was built in the 1860s and took its name from the Crimean War battle of 1854.

THE DARLINGTON–BARNARD CASTLE RAILWAY LINE crossed Newton Lane at Mount Pleasant level crossing. The rails were taken up soon after this photograph was taken in 1966.

SECTION NINE

Carmel Road and South Park

THE LONDON AND NORTH EASTERN RAILWAY COMPANY established two staff training schools in Darlington in former private houses, one at Faverdale Hall and the other, opened as an 'All-line Operating School', at 'Grantley', Carmel Road North.

THE DARLINGTON HARRIERS of 1904–5. The original Harriers, which hunted with a pack of beagles, was disbanded in 1889, when the pack was sold. The present Darlington Harriers, an athletic club, was formed in 1891, when the decision was taken to adopt the title of the former hunting club.

BY THE MIDDLE OF THE NINETEENTH CENTURY the problem of where to bury the dead of Darlington was a matter of 'grave' concern. The churchyards of St Cuthbert's and Holy Trinity were full and medical opinion at that time considered that the fumes rising from graves were a cause of disease. West Cemetery, then on the outskirts of the town, was opened in 1858, the first interment, of William Scaife of Brunswick Street, taking place on 16 June. This photograph, of 1890, shows the chapels with their original tall spire.

ONE OF A SERIES OF POSTCARDS which was commissioned by the North Eastern Railway Company and made available at stations and railway offices and works.

EDWARD DANIEL WALKER was born at Brighton in 1839. He joined the Stockton and Darlington Railway Company in 1852 but resigned in 1877 to lease the station bookstalls and provide refreshments for the North Eastern Railway Company. Elected to the council, he first became Mayor of Darlington in 1886, and again (after the sudden death of Alderman H. Thompson during his year of office) in 1892. In 1901 he presented the mayoress's chain of office to the town. In 1902, the year of Edward VII's coronation, although no longer a member of the council, he was invited to serve once more as Mayor of Darlington. Knighted in 1908, he was given the Freedom of the Borough ten years later. On his death in 1919, Sir E.D. Walker bequeathed £50,000 to the town for the provision of almshouses for the elderly, which were built on Coniscliffe Road.

When You Visit Darlington Park

(near the Banktop Station),

Call and have Tea in the Tea Gardens.

Centre of Park under Clock Tower, close Lawn Tennis Courts, Bowling Greens, and Boating on the River, etc.

= TEA TABLES =
on the Lawn.

Large Assortment of Best
Chocolates,
Biscuits,
Cakes,
Mineral Waters,
Tobacco & Cigars, etc.

MRS. T. LUNGLEY BETTS, Proprietress.

Private Address :
6, PRIBEND ROW, where all Orders for large and small parties will receive prompt attention.

AN INVITATION (OF 1900) TO TAKE TEA in Darlington Park (near Bank Top Station!). One wonders if Mrs T. Lungley Betts managed to negotiate a discount on the cost of her advertisement for the misspelling of her address.

A NEW RUSTIC TEA ROOM, designed by the borough engineer, was opened in South Park in June 1908 by the mayoress, Mrs Ada Starmer. Her husband, the mayor, Alderman C.W. Starmer, was regarded as 'the Napoleon of the newspaper world' in the north of England, being the Managing Director of *The Northern Echo* and many other newspapers.

THE ORIGINAL 'COTTAGE TEA ROOM' had been added to Park House in the 1860s. The cost of the verandah (£438) was partly met by the trustees of the park and partly by public subscription, organized by Joseph Pease.

THE TEA HOUSE, SOUTH PARK, DARLINGTON.

LITTLE HAS CHANGED since this photograph of the tea house and park house was taken, c. 1910.

THIS FOUNTAIN, now in South Park, was originally in the Botanical Gardens of Pierremont. It was presented to the town by a builder, Cuthbert Todd, in 1925. When Alderman Crooks ceremonially turned on its water supply, he expressed the hope that it 'would flow until the millenium'. Today, the fountain is dry and weeds flourish in its basin.

BOATING TOOK PLACE in this lake, below the park terrace, before 1921 when a new boating lake was constructed on the south side of Geneva Road (Parkside).

THE SOUTH PARK came into being as a result of a meeting held in May 1850, when the decision was taken to rent the land which formed part of the endowment of the Bellasis Charity from the Select Vestry of St Cuthbert's Church. Joseph Pease was prominent among those who donated money towards the cost of the laying out of the grounds and its landscaping. The park was administered by trustees until 1877, when Darlington Corporation acquired the land, the purchase money being given to the Queen Elizabeth Grammar School to provide scholarships.

ALTHOUGH THE ROCKS and rustic bridge are still *in situ* the present view of the western side of South Park is very different from that on this postcard, the area now being covered by a variety of shrubs and trees.

IT COULD BE ARGUED that this man, more than any other individual, has left his mark on the town and suburbs of Darlington. George Gordon Hoskins (1837–1911) came to Darlington to assist Alfred Waterhouse in the re-building of Backhouse's (now Barclay's) Bank on High Row. Establishing his own architectural practice in Northgate, he designed and built public buildings, offices, hotels and villas. These included the Greenbank Hospital, the Edward Pease Public Library, the North of England School Furnishing Company (now Lloyds Bank), the King's Head Hotel and Elm Ridge (built for John Pease), which is now a Methodist church.

FOR ALMOST FORTY YEARS, until their demolition in 1978, the cooling towers and chimneys of the town's power station dominated the skyline.

ACKNOWLEGEMENTS

I am grateful to the following people for the loan of material and permission to publish: Miss Joyce Banks • Mrs Jill Chatt • Mr Gordon Coates • Mr William Coates • Mr Stanley Dean, County Librarian, County Durham • Mr J.W. Fell Canon Alan Lazonby • Mrs Valerie Portass • Miss Audrey Reid Mrs Kate Singlehurst • Mr Edwin Smith • Mr Alan Suddes.

My especial thanks go to the staff of the Reference and Local History Libraries, Crown Street for their expertise and never-failing patience in answering queries.

Extra thanks go to Valerie Portass for her work in getting the manuscript ready for publication.

Without the help, support and local history knowledge of my wife Brenda this book might not have been published.